The Key Facts™ on

Tajikistan

Essential Information on Tajikistan

By Patrick W. Nee

The Internationalist®

www.internationalist.com

The Internationalist®

International Business, Investment, and Travel

Published by:

The Internationalist Publishing Company

96 Walter Street/ Suite 200

Boston, MA 02131, USA

Tel: 617-354-7722

www.internationalist.com

PN@internationalist.com

Table Of Contents

Chapter 1: Background

The Tajik people came under Russian rule in the 1860s and 1870s, but Russia's hold on Central Asia weakened following the Revolution of 1917. Bands of indigenous guerrillas (called "basmachi") fiercely contested Bolshevik control of the area, which was not fully reestablished until 1925. Tajikistan was first created as an autonomous republic within Uzbekistan in 1924, but the USSR designated Tajikistan a separate republic in 1929 and transferred to it much of present-day Sughd province. Ethnic Uzbeks form a substantial minority in Tajikistan. Tajikistan became independent in 1991 following the breakup of the Soviet Union, and experienced a civil war between regional factions from 1992 to 1997. Tajikistan endured several domestic security incidents during 2010-12, including armed conflict between government forces and local strongmen in the Rasht Valley and between government forces and criminal groups in Gorno-Badakhshan Autonomous Oblast. The country remains the poorest in the former Soviet sphere. Tajikistan became a member of the World Trade Organization in March 2013. However, its economy continues to face major challenges, including dependence on remittances from Tajikistanis working in Russia, pervasive corruption, and the major role narcotrafficking plays in the country's informal economy.

Chapter 2: Geography

Location:

Central Asia, west of China, south of Kyrgyzstan

Geographic coordinates:

39 00 N, 71 00 E

Map references:

Asia

Area:

total: 143,100 sq km

country comparison to the world: 96

land: 141,510 sq km

water: 2,590 sq km

Area - comparative:

slightly smaller than Wisconsin

Land boundaries:

total: 3,651 km

border countries: Afghanistan 1,206 km, China 414 km,

Kyrgyzstan 870 km, Uzbekistan 1,161 km

Coastline:

0 km (landlocked)

Maritime claims:

none (landlocked)

Climate:

midlatitude continental, hot summers, mild winters;
semiarid to polar in Pamir Mountains

Terrain:

Pamir and Alay Mountains dominate landscape; western Fergana Valley in north, Kofarnihon and Vakhsh Valleys in southwest

Elevation extremes:

lowest point: Syr Darya (Sirdaryo) 300 m

highest point: Qullai Ismoili Somoni 7,495 m

Natural resources:

hydropower, some petroleum, uranium, mercury, brown coal, lead, zinc, antimony, tungsten, silver, gold

Land use:

arable land: 5.96%

permanent crops: 0.91%

other: 93.13% (2011)

Irrigated land:

7,421 sq km (2009)

Total renewable water resources:

21.91 cu km (2011)

Freshwater withdrawal (domestic/industrial/agricultural):

total: 11.49 cu km/yr (6%/4%/91%)

per capita: 1,740 cu m/yr (2006)

Natural hazards:

earthquakes; floods

Environment - current issues:

inadequate sanitation facilities; increasing levels of soil salinity; industrial pollution; excessive pesticides

Environment - international agreements:

party to: Biodiversity, Climate Change, Climate Change-Kyoto Protocol, Desertification, Environmental Modification, Ozone Layer Protection, Wetlands

signed, but not ratified: none of the selected agreements

Geography - note:

landlocked; mountainous region dominated by the Trans-Alay Range in the north and the Pamirs in the southeast; highest point, Qullai Ismoili Somoni (formerly Communism Peak), was the tallest mountain in the former USSR

Chapter 3: People and Society

Nationality:

noun: Tajikistani(s)

adjective: Tajikistani

Ethnic groups:

Tajik 79.9%, Uzbek 15.3%, Russian 1.1%, Kyrgyz 1.1%, other 2.6% (2000 census)

note: estimates of Uzbek proportion can range as high as 25% depending on how mixed Tajik-Uzbek families (largely in border areas) are counted

Languages:

Tajik (official), Russian widely used in government and business

Religions:

Sunni Muslim 85%, Shia Muslim 5%, other 10% (2003 est.)

Population:

8,051,512 (July 2014 est.)

country comparison to the world: 97

Age structure:

0-14 years: 33% (male 1,352,150/female 1,304,615)

15-24 years: 20.1% (male 819,936/female 796,211)

25-54 years: 38.9% (male 1,547,863/female 1,586,218)

55-64 years: 3.2% (male 178,161/female 210,616)

65 years and over: 3.2% (male 107,137/female 148,605)

(2014 est.)

Dependency ratios:

total dependency ratio: 64.1 %

youth dependency ratio: 58.9 %

elderly dependency ratio: 5.2 %

potential support ratio: 19.1 (2013)

Median age:

total: 23.5 years

male: 23 years

female: 24 years (2014 est.)

Population growth rate:

1.75% (2014 est.)

country comparison to the world: 69

Birth rate:

24.99 births/1,000 population (2014 est.)

country comparison to the world: 56

Death rate:

6.28 deaths/1,000 population (2014 est.)

country comparison to the world: 158

Net migration rate:

-1.17 migrant(s)/1,000 population (2014 est.)

country comparison to the world: 152

Urbanization:

urban population: 26.5% of total population (2011)

rate of urbanization 1.66% annual rate of change (2010-15 est.)

Major urban areas - population:

DUSHANBE (capital) 704,000 (2009)

Sex ratio:

at birth: 1.05 male(s)/female

0-14 years: 1.04 male(s)/female

15-24 years: 1.03 male(s)/female

25-54 years: 0.98 male(s)/female

55-64 years: 0.99 male(s)/female

65 years and over: 0.73 male(s)/female

total population: 0.99 male(s)/female (2014 est.)

Mother's mean age at first birth:

22.8

note: median age at first birth among women 25-29 (2010 est.)

Maternal mortality rate:

65 deaths/100,000 live births (2010)

country comparison to the world: 94

Infant mortality rate:

> total: 35.03 deaths/1,000 live births
>
> country comparison to the world: 64
>
> male: 39.42 deaths/1,000 live births
>
> female: 30.42 deaths/1,000 live births (2014 est.)

Life expectancy at birth:

> total population: 67.06 years
>
> country comparison to the world: 166
>
> male: 63.96 years
>
> female: 70.32 years (2014 est.)

Total fertility rate:

> 2.76 children born/woman (2014 est.)
>
> country comparison to the world: 71

Contraceptive prevalence rate:

> 27.9% (2012)

Health expenditures:

> 5.8% of GDP (2011)
>
> country comparison to the world: 117

Physicians density:

> 1.9 physicians/1,000 population (2011)

Hospital bed density:

> 5.5 beds/1,000 population (2011)

Drinking water source:

improved:

urban: 91.8% of population

rural: 56.5% of population

total: 65.9% of population

unimproved:

urban: 8.2% of population

rural: 43.5% of population

total: 34.1% of population (2011 est.)

Sanitation facility access:

improved:

urban: 95.4% of population

rural: 94.4% of population

total: 94.7% of population

unimproved:

urban: 4.6% of population

rural: 5.6% of population

total: 5.3% of population (2011 est.)

HIV/AIDS - adult prevalence rate:

0.3% (2012)

country comparison to the world: 94

HIV/AIDS - people living with HIV/AIDS:

11,900 (2012)

country comparison to the world: 97

HIV/AIDS - deaths:

500 (2012)

country comparison to the world: 89

Major infectious diseases:

degree of risk: high

food or waterborne diseases: bacterial diarrhea, hepatitis A, and typhoid fever

vectorborne disease: malaria (2013)

Obesity - adult prevalence rate:

8.6% (2008)

country comparison to the world: 136

Children under the age of 5 underweight:

15% (2007)

country comparison to the world: 49

Education expenditures:

3.9% of GDP (2011)

country comparison to the world: 114

Literacy:

definition: age 15 and over can read and write

total population: 99.7%

male: 99.8%

female: 99.6% (2011 est.)

School life expectancy (primary to tertiary education):

total: 11 years

male: 12 years

female: 10 years (2011)

Child labor – children ages 5-14:

<u>total number:</u> 164,432

<u>percentage:</u> 10 % (2005 est.)

Unemployment, youth ages 15-24:

<u>total:</u> 16.7%

<u>country comparison to the world</u>: 77

<u>male</u>: 19.2%

<u>female</u>: 13.7% (2009)

Chapter 4: Government and Key Leaders

Country name:

conventional long form: Republic of Tajikistan

conventional short form: Tajikistan

local long form: Jumhurii Tojikiston

local short form: Tojikiston

former: Tajik Soviet Socialist Republic

Government type:

republic

Capital:

name: Dushanbe

geographic coordinates: 38 33 N, 68 46 E

time difference: UTC+5 (10 hours ahead of Washington, DC during Standard Time)

Administrative divisions:

2 provinces (viloyatho, singular - viloyat), 1 autonomous province* (viloyati mukhtor), 1 capital region** (viloyati poytakht), and 1 area referred to as Districts Under Republic Administration***; Dushanbe**, Khatlon (Qurghonteppa), Kuhistoni Badakhshon [Gorno-Badakhshan]* (Khorugh), Nohiyahoi Tobei Jumhuri***, Sughd (Khujand)

Independence:

9 September 1991 (from the Soviet Union)

National holiday:

Independence Day (or National Day), 9 September (1991)

Constitution:

several previous; latest adopted 6 November 1994;
amended 1999, 2003 (2009)

Legal system:

civil law system

International law organization participation:

has not submitted an ICJ jurisdiction declaration; accepts
ICCt jurisdiction

Suffrage:

18 years of age; universal

Executive branch:

chief of state: President Emomali RAHMON (since 6
November 1994; head of state and Supreme Assembly
chairman since 19 November 1992)

head of government: Prime Minister Qohir RASULZODA
(since 23 November 2013); First Deputy Prime Minister
Davlatali SAIDOV (since 19 November 2013)

cabinet: Council of Ministers appointed by the president,
approved by the Supreme Assembly

electionspresident elected by popular vote for a seven-year
term (technically eligible for two terms); election last held
on 6 November 2013 (next to be held in November 2020);
prime minister appointed by the president

election results: Emomali RAHMON reelected president;
percent of vote - Emomali RAHMON 83.9%, Ismoil
TALBAKOV 5%, other 11.1%

Legislative branch:

bicameral Supreme Assembly or Majlisi Oli consists of the
National Assembly (upper chamber) or Majlisi Milli (34
seats; 25 members selected by local deputies, 8 appointed
by the president; 1 seat reserved for the former president;
members serve five-year terms) and the Assembly of
Representatives (lower chamber) or Majlisi
Namoyandagon (63 seats; 41 members elected through
constituencies, 22 members elected through party selection;
members serve five-year terms)

elections: National Assembly - last held on 28 February
2010 (next to be held in February 2015); Assembly of
Representatives - last held on 28 February 2010 (next to be
held in February 2015)

election results: National Assembly - percent of vote by
party - NA; seats by party - NA; Assembly of
Representatives - percent of vote by party - PDPT 71%,
IRPT 8.2%, CPT 7%, APT 5.1%, PERT 5.1%, other 3.6%;
seats by party - PDPT 55, IRPT 2, CPT 2, APT 2, PERT 2

Judicial branch:

Highest court(s): Supreme Court (consists of the chairman, deputy chairmen, and 34 judges organized into civil, criminal, and military chambers); Constitutional Court (consists of the court chairman, vice-president, and 5 judges); High Economic Court (consists 16 judicial positions)

Judge selection and term of offfice: Supreme Court, Constitutional Court, and High Economic Court judges nominated by the president of the republic and approved by the National Assembly; judges of all three courts appointed for 10-year renewable terms with no limit on terms, but last appointment must occur before the age of 65

subordinate courts: regional and district courts; Dushanbe City Court; viloyat (province level) courts; Court of Gorno-Badakhshan Autonomous Region

Political parties and leaders:

Agrarian Party of Tajikistan or APT [Amir QARAQULOV]

Communist Party of Tajikistan or CPT [Shodi SHABDOLOV]

Democratic Party of Tajikistan [Saidjafar ISMONOV]

Islamic Revival Party of Tajikistan or IRPT [Muhiddin KABIRI]

Party of Economic Reform of Tajikistan or PERT
[Olimjon BOBOEV]

People's Democratic Party of Tajikistan or PDPT
[Emomali RAHMON]

Social Democratic Party of Tajikistan or SDPT
[Rahmatullo ZOYIROV]

Socialist Party of Tajikistan or SPT [Abduhalim
GHAFOROV]

Political pressure groups and leaders:

influential religious leader Akbar TURAJONZODA

unregistered Youth Party of Tajikistan [Izzat AMON]

unregistered opposition group Guruhi-24 (Group-24)
[Umarali QUVVATOV]

Vatandor (Patriot) Movement [Dodojon
ATOVULLOEV]

unregistered presidential candidate of Union of
Reformist Forces of Tajikistan Oynihol
BOBONAZAROVA

unregistered New Tajikistan party [Zayd SAIDOV]

International organization participation:

ADB, CICA, CIS, CSTO, EAEC, EAPC, EBRD, ECO, FAO, G-
77, GCTU, IAEA, IBRD, ICAO, ICC (NGOs), ICRM, IDA, IDB,
IFAD, IFC, IFRCS, ILO, IMF, Interpol, IOC, IOM, IPU, ISO
(correspondent), ITSO, ITU, MIGA, MINUSMA, NAM
(observer), OIC, OPCW, OSCE, PFP, SCO, UN, UNCTAD,

UNESCO, UNIDO, UNWTO, UPU, WCO, WFTU (NGOs), WHO, WIPO, WMO, WTO

Diplomatic representation in the US:

chief of mission: Ambassador Nuriddin SHAMSOV (since 30 July 2012)

chancery: 1005 New Hampshire Avenue NW, Washington, DC 20037

telephone: [1] (202) 223-6090

FAX: [1] (202) 223-6091

Diplomatic representation from the US:

chief of mission: Ambassador Susan M. ELLIOTT (since 25 July 2012)

embassy: 109-A Ismoili Somoni Avenue, Dushanbe 734019

mailing address: 7090 Dushanbe Place, Dulles, VA 20189

telephone: [992] (37) 229-20-00

FAX: [992] (37) 229-20-50

Key Leaders:

Pres.	Emomali RAHMON
Prime Min.	Qohir RASULZODA
First Dep. Prime Min.	Davlatali SAIDOV
Dep. Prime Min.	Murodali ALIMARDON
Dep. Prime Min.	Azim IBROHIM
Dep. Prime Min.	Marhabo JABBOROVA
Min. of Agriculture	Qosim QOSIMOV
Min. of Culture	Shamsiddin ORUMBEKOV
Min. of Defense	Sherali MIRZO, *Lt. Gen.*
Min. of Economic Development &	Sharif RAHIMZODA

Trade

Min. of Education & Science	Nuriddin SAIDOV
Min. of Energy & Water Resources	Usmonali USMONOV
Min. of Finance	Abdusalom QURBONOV
Min. of Foreign Affairs	Sirojidin ASLOV
Min. of Health & Public Safety	Nusratullo SALIMOV
Min. of Industry & New Technologies	Shavkat BOBOEV
Min. of Internal Affairs	Ramazon RAHIMZODA
Min. of Justice	Rustam MENGLIEV
Min. of Labor, Migration, & Public Employment	Sumangul TAGHOEVA
Min. of Transport	Khayrullo ASOEV
Chmn., State Committee for National Security	Saymumin YATIMOV, *Lt. Gen.*
Prosecutor Gen.	Sherhon SALIMZODA
Dir., Drug Control Agency	Rustam NAZAROV, *Lt. Gen.*
Chmn., National Bank of Tajikistan	Abdujabbor SHIRINOV
Ambassador to the US	Nuriddin SHAMSOV
Permanent Representative to the UN, New York	Mahmadamin MAHMADAMINOV

Flag description:

three horizontal stripes of red (top), a wider stripe of white, and green; a gold crown surmounted by seven gold, five-pointed stars is located in the center of the white stripe; red represents the sun, victory, and the unity of the nation, white stands for purity, cotton, and mountain snows, while green is the color of Islam and the bounty of nature; the crown symbolizes the Tajik people; the seven stars signify the Tajik magic number "seven" - a symbol of perfection and the embodiment of happiness

National symbol(s):

crown surmounted by seven, five-pointed stars

National anthem:

name: "Surudi milli" (National Anthem)

lyrics/music: Gulnazar KELDI/Suleiman YUDAKOV

note: adopted 1991; after the fall of the Soviet Union, Tajikistan kept the music of the anthem from its time as a Soviet republic but adopted new lyrics

Chapter 5: Economy

Economy - overview:

Tajikistan has one of the lowest per capita GDPs among the 15 former Soviet republics. The 1992-1997 civil war severely damaged an already weak economic infrastructure and caused a sharp decline in industrial and agricultural production. Because of a lack of employment opportunities in Tajikistan, more than one million Tajik citizens work abroad - roughly 90% in Russia - supporting families in Tajikistan through remittances. Less than 7% of the land area is arable and cotton is the most important crop. Until 2008, cotton production was closely monitored and controlled by the government. In the wake of the National Bank of Tajikistan's admission in December 2007 that it had directed the AgroInvestBank to improperly lend money to politically connected investors in the cotton sector, the IMF canceled its stand-by assistance program in Tajikistan. As part of the Tajik government's subsequent reforms, over a half billion dollars in farmer debt has been forgiven. In 2008 Tajikistan passed new law authorizing farmers to decide for themselves what crops to grow, and this has resulted in a gradual decrease in cotton output. Tajikistan imports approximately 60% of its food, most of which comes by rail. Uzbekistan closed one of the rail lines into Tajikistan in late 2011, hampering the transit of goods to and from the southern part of the country. As a result, food and fuel prices increased to the highest levels since 2002. Mineral resources include silver, gold, uranium, and tungsten. Industry consists mainly of small obsolete factories in food processing and light industry, substantial hydropower facilities, and a large aluminum plant - currently operating below 25% of capacity. Electricity output expanded with the completion of the Sangtuda-1 hydropower dam - finished in 2009 with Russian investment. The smaller Sangtuda-2 hydropower dam, built with Iranian investment, began operating in 2012 at a limited capacity. The Tajik government is tens of millions of dollars in arrears for both Sangtuda dams, and Sangtuda-2 has been closed for "maintenance" since January 2014. The government is pinning its drive for energy independence on completion of the Roghun dam, which is scheduled for mid-2014. In 2010, the government began a coerced sale of shares in the Roghun enterprise to its population, ultimately raising over $180 million before stopping under intense criticism from international donors, but the dam is likely to cost billions of dollars. The World Bank funded two feasibility studies (technical-economic, and social-environmental) for the dam. If built according to plan, Roghun will be the tallest dam in the world, will operate year around, and will significantly expand Tajikistan's electricity output. In 2013, the Tajik government finalized an agreement to import one million tons of fuel and oil products from Russia each year, at reduced prices. Tajikistan's economic situation remains fragile due to uneven implementation of structural reforms, corruption, weak governance, seasonal power shortages, and its large external debt burden.

GDP (purchasing power parity):

$19.2 billion (2013 est.)

country comparison to the world: 137

$17.88 billion (2012 est.)

$16.63 billion (2011 est.)

note: data are in 2013 US dollars

GDP (official exchange rate):

$8.513 billion (2013 est.)

GDP - real growth rate:

7.4% (2013 est.)

country comparison to the world: 18

7.5% (2012 est.)

7.4% (2011 est.)

GDP - per capita (PPP):

$2,300 (2013 est.)

country comparison to the world: 189

$2,200 (2012 est.)

$2,100 (211 est.)

note: data are in 2013 US dollars

Gross national saving:

12.4% of GDP (2013 est.)

country comparison to the world: 125

17.8% of GDP (2012 est.)

10% of GDP (2011 est.)

GDP – composition, by end use:

household consumption: 97%

government consumption: 12%

investment in fixed capital: 14%

investment in inventories: 6.7%

exports of goods and services: 13.7%

imports of goods and services: -48.5% (2013 est.)

GDP - composition by sector of origin:

agriculture: 21.1%

industry: 23.2%

services: 55.7% (2013 est.)

Agriculture – products:

cotton, grain, fruits, grapes, vegetables; cattle, sheep, goats

Industries:

aluminum, cement, vegetable oil

Industrial production growth rate:

3.9% (2013 est.)

country comparison to the world: 76

Labor force:

2.209 million (2013 est.)

country comparison to the world: 118

Labor force - by occupation:

agriculture: 46.5%

industry: 10.7%

services: 42.8% (2013 est.)

Unemployment rate:

2.5% (2013 est.)

country comparison to the world: 20

2.5% (2012 est.)

note: official rates; actual unemployment is much higher

Population below poverty line:

35.6% (2013 est.)

Household income or consumption by percentage share:

lowest 10%: NA%

highest 10%: NA% (2009 est.)

Distribution of family income - Gini index:

32.6 (2006)

country comparison to the world: 104

34.7 (1998)

Budget:

revenues: $2.425 billion

expenditures: $2.423 billion (2013 est.)

Taxes and other revenues:

28.5% of GDP (2013 est.)

country comparison to the world: 102

Budget surplus (+) or deficit (-):

0% of GDP (2013 est.)

country comparison to the world: 43

Public debt:

6.5% of GDP

country comparison to the world: 154

Inflation rate (consumer prices):

3.7% (2013 est.)

country comparison to the world: 124

5.8% (2012 est.)

Central bank discount rate:

4.8% (31 December 2013 est.)

country comparison to the world: 54

6.5% (31 December 2012 est.)

Commercial bank prime lending rate:

22% (31 December 2013 est.)

country comparison to the world: 29

17.13% (31 December 2012 est.)

Stock of narrow money:

$1.044 billion (31 December 2013 est.)

country comparison to the world: 150

$1.191 billion (31 December 2012 est.)

Stock of broad money:

$2.033 billion (31 December 2013 est.)

country comparison to the world: 149

$1.555 billion (31 December 2012 est.)

Stock of domestic credit:

$1.611 billion (31 December 2013 est.)

country comparison to the world: 140

$1.196 billion (31 December 2012 est.)

Current account balance:

-$330 million (2013 est.)

country comparison to the world: 92

-$246.2 million (2012 est.)

Exports:

$1.163 billion (2013 est.)

country comparison to the world: 154

$826.6 million (2012 est.)

Exports - commodities:

aluminum, electricity, cotton, fruits, vegetable oil, textiles

Exports - partners:

Turkey 40.7%, Russia 10.6%, Iran 9.9%, Afghanistan 8.7%, China 7.4%, Kazakhstan 7.4%, Switzerland 6.6% (2012 est.)

Imports:

$4.121 billion (2013 est.)

country comparison to the world: 137

$3.778 billion (2012 est.)

Imports - commodities:

petroleum products, aluminum oxide, machinery and equipment, foodstuffs

Imports - partners:

Russia 22%, Kazakhstan 15.2%, China 14.5%, Lithuania 4.7%, Kyrgyzstan 4.4%, Turkey 4.4%, Iran 4.3% (2012 est.)

Reserves of foreign exchange and gold:

$1.072 billion (31 December 2013 est.)

country comparison to the world: 133

$972 million (31 December 2012 est.)

Debt - external:

$2.162 billion (31 December 2013 est.)

country comparison to the world: 142

$3.439 billion (31 December 2012 est.)

Stock of direct foreign investment – at home:

$2.272 billion (31 December 2013 est.)

country comparison to the world: 97

Stock of foreign investment – abroad:

$16.3 billion (31 December 2009 est.)

Exchange rates:

Tajikistani somoni (TJS) per US dollar -

4.76 (2013 est.)

4.76 (2012 est.)

4.379 (2010 est.)

4.1428 (2009)

3.4563 (2008)

Chapter 6: Energy

Electricity - production:

17.09 billion kWh (2013 est.)

country comparison to the world: 78

Electricity - consumption:

16.09 billion kWh (2013 est.)

country comparison to the world: 75

Electricity - exports:

1 billion kWh (2013 est.)

country comparison to the world: 57

Electricity - imports:

300.5 million kWh (2012 est.)

country comparison to the world: 81

Electricity - installed generating capacity:

4.476 million kW (2013 est.)

country comparison to the world: 77

Electricity - from fossil fuels:

9% of total installed capacity (2013 est.)

country comparison to the world: 197

Electricity - from nuclear fuels:

0% of total installed capacity (2013 est.)

country comparison to the world: 185

Electricity - from hydroelectric plants:

91% of total installed capacity (2013 est.)

country comparison to the world: 12

Electricity - from other renewable sources:

0% of total installed capacity (2013 est.)

country comparison to the world: 126

Crude oil - production:

553 bbl/day (2013 est.)

country comparison to the world: 114

Crude oil - exports:

0 bbl/day (2013 est.)

country comparison to the world: 188

Crude oil - imports:

0 bbl/day (2013 est.)

country comparison to the world: 125

Crude oil - proved reserves:

12 million bbl (1 January 2013 es)

country comparison to the world: 88

Refined petroleum products - production:

400 bbl/day

country comparison to the world: 113

Refined petroleum products - consumption:

20,090 bbl/day (2013 est.)

country comparison to the world: 127

Refined petroleum products - exports:

500 bbl/day (2013 est.)

country comparison to the world: 114

Refined petroleum products - imports:

20,090 bbl/day (2013 est.)

country comparison to the world:106

Natural gas - production:

3.928 million cu m (2013 est.)

country comparison to the world: 94

Natural gas - consumption:

3.928 million cu m (2013 est.)

country comparison to the world: 113

Natural gas - exports:

0 cu m (2013 est.)

country comparison to the world: 189

Natural gas - imports:

0 cu m (2013 est.)

country comparison to the world: 134

Natural gas - proved reserves:

5.663 billion cu m (1 January 2013 es)

country comparison to the world: 92

Carbon dioxide emissions from consumption of energy:

2.618 million Mt (2013 est.)

country comparison to the world: 142

Chapter 7: Communications

Telephones - main lines in use:

393,000 (2012)

country comparison to the world: 106

Telephones - mobile cellular:

6.528 million (2012)

country comparison to the world: 98

Telephone system:

general assessment: foreign investment in the telephone system has resulted in major improvements; conversion of the existing fixed network from analogue to digital was completed in 2012

domestic: fixed line availability has not changed significantly since 1998 while mobile cellular subscribership, aided by competition among multiple operators, has expanded rapidly; coverage now extends to all major cities and towns

international: country code - 992; linked by cable and microwave radio relay to other CIS republics and by leased connections to the Moscow international gateway switch; Dushanbe linked by Intelsat to international gateway switch in Ankara (Turkey); satellite earth stations - 3 (2 Intelsat and 1 Orbita) (2011)

Broadcast media:

state-run TV broadcaster transmits nationally on 4 stations and regionally on 4 stations; 11 independent TV stations broadcast locally and regionally; some households are able to receive Russian and other foreign stations via cable and satellite; state-run radio broadcaster operates Radio Tajikistan, Voice of Dushanbe, and several regional stations; a small number of independent radio stations (2010)

Internet country code:

.tj

Internet hosts:

6,258 (2012)

country comparison to the world: 142

Internet users:

700,000 (2009)

country comparison to the world: 110

Chapter 8: Transportation

Airports:

 24 (2013)

 country comparison to the world: 131

Airports - with paved runways:

 total: 17

 over 3,047 m: 2

 2,438 to 3,047 m: 4

 1,524 to 2,437 m: 5

 914 to 1,523 m: 3

 under 914 m: 3 (2013)

Airports - with unpaved runways:

 total: 7

 1,524 to 2,437 m: 1

 914 to 1,523 m: 1

 under 914 m: 5 (2013)

Pipelines:

 gas 549 km; oil 38 km (2013)

Railways:

 total: 680 km

 country comparison to the world: 103

 broad gauge: 680 km 1.520-m gauge (2008)

Roadways:

 total: 27,767 km (2000)

 country comparison to the world: 98

Waterways:

200 km (along Vakhsh River) (2011)

country comparison to the world: 99

Chapter 9: Military

Military branches:

Ground Forces, Air and Air Defense Forces, Mobile
Forces (2013)

Military service age and obligation:

18-27 years of age for compulsory or voluntary military
service; 2-year conscript service obligation; males required
to undergo compulsory military training between ages 16
and 55; males can enroll in military schools from at least
age 15 (2012)

Manpower available for military service:

males age 16-49: 2,012,790

females age 16-49: 2,020,618 (2010 est.)

Manpower fit for military service:

males age 16-49: 1,490,267

females age 16-49: 1,675,083 (2010 est.)

Manpower reaching militarily significant age annually:

male: 76,430

female: 74,038 (2010 est.)

Chapter 10: Transnational Issues

Disputes - international:

in 2006, China and Tajikistan pledged to commence demarcation of the revised boundary agreed to in the delimitation of 2002; talks continue with Uzbekistan to delimit border and remove minefields; disputes in Isfara Valley delay delimitation with Kyrgyzstan

Refugees and internally displaced persons:

stateless persons: 2,300 (2012)

Illicit drugs:

major transit country for Afghan narcotics bound for Russian and, to a lesser extent, Western European markets; limited illicit cultivation of opium poppy for domestic consumption; Tajikistan seizes roughly 80% of all drugs captured in Central Asia and stands third worldwide in seizures of opiates (heroin and raw opium); significant consumer of opiates

Map of Tajikistan

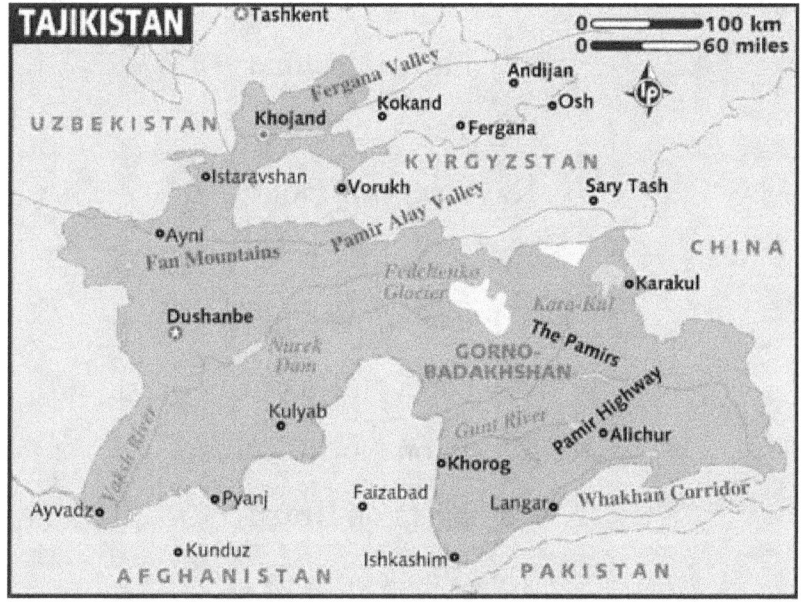

Other Key Facts™ Titles

Key Facts on Syria

Key Facts on China

Key Facts on Qatar

Key Facts on India

Key Facts on Germany

Key Facts on Argentina

Key Facts on Russia

Key Facts on North Korea

Key Facts on Brazil

Key Facts on Italy

Key Facts on the United Arab Emirates

Key Facts on the European Union

Key Facts on Pakistan

Key Facts on Saudi Arabia

Key Facts on Cyprus

Key Facts on Iran

Key Facts on Afghanistan

Key Facts on Iraq

Key Facts on Indonesia

Key Facts on South Korea

Key Facts on France

Key Facts on the United Kingdom

Key Facts on Egypt

Key Facts on Israel

All Key Facts™ Titles are Available at

www.Amazon.com

THE INTERNATIONALIST®

2014

WWW.INTERNATIONALIST.COM